HAMBU...
THE CITY AT A ...

Binnenalster
Hamburg's 'inner' lake ...
made reservoir. Its shores are the city's urban
playground, hosting events and festivals.

Fairmont Hotel Vier Jahreszeiten
First opened in 1897, then extended in the
1930s and the 1950s, the 'Four Seasons'
is one of the grandest of the fin-de-siècle
white mansions that line the Binnenalster.
Neuer Jungfernstieg 9-14, T 34 940

Rathaus
Martin Haller's city hall is the focal point of
Mitte. Its elaborate 1897 facade features 20
busts of the kaisers and a riot of adornment.
Rathausmarkt 1, T 428 312 064

HafenCity
The ambitious docklands redevelopment
is attracting the world's architectural elite.
See p028

St Nikolai-Kirche
At 147m, the spire of this neo-Gothic church
made it the world's tallest building in 1874.
Bombed to a shell during WWII, the ruins are
preserved as a monument to victims of war.
Willy-Brandt-Strasse 60, T 371 125

Laeiszhalle
Erwin Meerwein and Martin Haller's 1908 neo-
baroque concert hall has hosted Maria Callas,
Richard Strauss, Yehudi Menuhin and more.
Johannes-Brahms-Platz, T 357 6660

Michaeliskirche
This much-loved icon's 132m-high bell tower
and distinctive clock face are said to have
guided sailors to the city's shores. The views
from the summit are wonderful.
Englische Planke 1, T 376 780

INTRODUCTION
THE CHANGING FACE OF THE URBAN SCENE

Bourgeois, cosmopolitan and a touch aloof, Hamburg is not an in-your-face city, a fact credited to its thriving professional classes. For the visitor, this does mean that an extra effort is needed, but dig beneath the surface and it will quickly become apparent why few Germans cherish their hometown as much as Hamburgers do. Its location between the Elbe and Alster rivers, and its pleasant canals, deep blue lakes, thousands of bridges and expanses of green space make it a beautiful city. It is also among Europe's wealthiest, many of its copious millionaires filling their coffers through one of the world's busiest commercial ports. Now Hamburg has established itself as Germany's media capital as well, home to the publishing giants Stern, Die Zeit and Spiegel (see p070). Rather than losing residents, as it did for much of the early 20th century, the place is booming, its population expected to rise seven per cent by 2040.

Unlike other European metropolises that for years turned their backs on the docks, Hamburg has always embraced them. The far-reaching, mixed-tenure development HafenCity (see p028) is the latest stage in this process, principally conceived to accommodate urban immigrants, and is a blank canvas that is attracting the top architects in the world. Although OMA's Science Centre – a giant glass doughnut – was shelved, little else has been affected by the global financial crisis. With penthouses here selling as fast as they can be built, Hamburg's future looks as buoyant as ever.

ESSENTIAL INFO

FACTS, FIGURES AND USEFUL ADDRESSES

TOURIST OFFICE
Hauptbahnhof
T 3005 1701
www.hamburg-tourism.de

TRANSPORT
Airport transfer to city centre
S-Bahn trains to the Hauptbahnhof depart
regularly. The journey takes 25 minutes
www.hvv.de
Car hire
Europcar
T 378 6220
Ferry service
www.hadag.de
S-Bahn/U-Bahn
Trains run from roughly 4.30am to
12.30am, and for 24 hours at weekends
Taxis
Hansa-Taxi
T 211 211
Travel card
A five-day bus and train pass costs €38.50

EMERGENCY SERVICES
Ambulance/fire
T 112
Police
T 110
Late-night pharmacy (check for rota)
www.apothekerkammer-hamburg.de

CONSULATES AND EMBASSIES
British Embassy
Wilhelmstrasse 70/71
Berlin
T 030 204 570
www.gov.uk/government/world/germany
US Consulate-General
Alsterufer 27-28
T 4117 1100
hamburg.usconsulate.gov

POSTAL SERVICES
Post office
Hachmannplatz 13
T 018 023 333
www.deutschepost.de
Shipping
UPS
T 080 0882 6630

BOOKS
The Beatles in Hamburg by
Spencer Leigh (Omnibus Press)
Hamburg: A Cultural History by
Matthew Jefferies (Interlink Books)
**Hamburg: Architecture of
a Changing City** (Jovis Verlag)
On the Natural History of Destruction
by WG Sebald (Penguin)

WEBSITES
Architecture
a-tour.de
Newspaper
www.thelocal.de

EVENTS
Filmfest Hamburg
www.filmfesthamburg.de/en
Reeperbahn Festival
www.reeperbahnfestival.com

COST OF LIVING
Taxi from Hamburg Airport to Mitte
€24
Cappuccino
€3
Packet of cigarettes
€5.50
Daily newspaper
€1.20
Bottle of champagne
€80

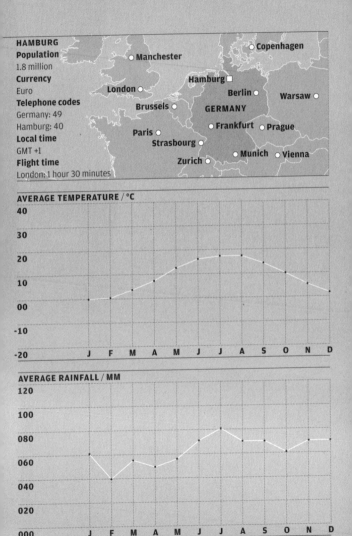

HAMBURG
Population
1.8 million
Currency
Euro
Telephone codes
Germany: 49
Hamburg: 40
Local time
GMT +1
Flight time
London: 1 hour 30 minutes

AVERAGE TEMPERATURE / °C

40
30
20
10
00
-10
-20

J F M A M J J A S O N D

AVERAGE RAINFALL / MM

120
100
080
060
040
020
000

J F M A M J J A S O N D

NEIGHBOURHOODS
THE AREAS YOU NEED TO KNOW AND WHY

To help you navigate the city, we've chosen the most interesting districts (see below and the map inside the back cover) and colour-coded our featured venues, according to their location; those venues that are outside these areas are not coloured.

EIMSBÜTTEL
Park-filled Eimsbüttel has benefited from the overflow of hip 'hoods Schanze and St Pauli and grown into a media and creative hub. There are bustling hangouts along Weidenallee and Max-Brauer-Allee, such as Bar Rossi (No 279, T 433 421), and fine local cuisine at Bistrot Vienna (see p030).

ST GEORG
This villagey gay district has shops, clubs and cinemas clustered around Steindamm, while Lange Reihe hosts boutiques, bars and bistros such as Cox (No 68, T 249 422) amid red-brick residences. The area abuts Aussenalster lake, which is skirted by boat clubs, gracious white mansions and swanky bars including A Mora (see p048).

MITTE WEST
Binnenalster lake is the focal point of the blue-blooded swathe of the centre. Other draws are the Italianate Alsterarkaden, its graceful arches providing shelter to high-end shops and terrace cafés, and the huge Planten un Blomen park to the north, which is a triumph of botanical design.

EPPENDORF/HARVESTEHUDE
Bourgeois Eppendorf offers retail therapy in the form of destination interiors stores such as Roomservice (see p085). Lining Isestrasse, the city's finest neo-baroque mansions are the backdrop to a great food market. Early 20th-century splendour can be found on Hochallee in Harvestehude.

HAFENCITY
Cranes, canals and big-name architecture mark this vast docklands project that is finding new uses for century-old red-brick storerooms. HafenCity's showpiece is Herzog & de Meuron's Elbphilharmonie (see p071), which places an iceberg-like structure on top of a massive warehouse.

SCHANZE
Often considered to be the northern part of St Pauli, Schanze, which encompasses Schanzenviertel and Karolinenviertel, is a pocket of left-of-centre hipness. Funky eateries (see p052) and fashion start-ups line Marktstrasse and its cross streets, and Sternschanzenpark hosts the Mövenpick Hotel (see p016) in a former water tower.

MITTE EAST
East of the Alsterfleet canal lies the city's retail core and the grandiose Rathaus (see p009). Further east, in Kontorhausviertel, are splendid examples of 1920s vernacular clinker-brick office buildings, including the Chilehaus (see p013) and the neighbouring Sprinkenhof and Mohlenhof.

ALTONA/ST PAULI
There's more to this area than the famous Reeperbahn. Bold public spaces and new architecture, such as Dockland (see p010), are springing up by the river. Chilled-out, multicultural Altona, with its gourmet delis and cafés (see p025), is in stark contrast to its gritty, rock'n'roll neighbour, St Pauli.

LANDMARKS

THE SHAPE OF THE CITY SKYLINE

The waterways of Hamburg are its signposts. Binnenalster lake forms the northern boundary of Mitte East and West, the city's historic core that is dominated by the rambling, neo-Renaissance Rathaus (Rathausmarkt 1, T 428 312 064), a huge fairy-tale castle. The Alsterfleet canal divides Mitte in half and the Elbe river marks its southern edge. However, the mammoth 157-hectare mixed-use HafenCity project, which is being developed in stages until 2025, has annexed the old warehouse district on an island in the Elbe, and will expand the centre of Hamburg by 40 per cent. Its flagship building, the Elbphilharmonie (see p071), has now risen beside the designer lofts, offices (see p067), retail and leisure facilities.

Waterside development is also being embraced further to the east. Dockland (see p010) is the modern beacon for the old port, an industrial slab of land where fish-packing warehouses sit next to (or house) stylish restaurants such as Henssler & Henssler (see p036). Inland from here are the hip districts of Altona and St Pauli. It is often claimed that, approaching from Mitte, Michaeliskirche (Englische Planke 1, T 376 780) is the gateway to the city's famous red-light district. However, it's not until you can spy the massed concrete of the WWII bunker Flakturm IV (see p014) to the north, or the top of the teetering-as-if-drunk Tanzende Türme (see p012), that you are approaching the chaotic main drag, Reeperbahn.
For full addresses, see Resources.

Dockland

Built entirely on the water by Hamburg
architects Bothe Richter Teherani (BRT),
this sharp-angled steel-and-glass office
building projects 40m over the river
like a ship's prow. Worth the climb is the
rooftop terrace, which boasts great views
of the waterside and the Elbberg Campus
(see p062), also designed by BRT.
*Van-der-Smissen-Strasse 9,
www.dockland-hamburg.de*

Tanzende Türme

Located at the busy intersection of St Pauli, Altona and the Reeperbahn, the 'Dancing Towers', another project by BRT, became the city's most conspicuous architectural statement in 2011. The 90m and 80m high-rises lean towards and then shy away from each other, slanting by up to 3m from the vertical, giving the impression of a flirting couple. It's a reference to the infamous 19th-century Trichter dancehall that was once here, and to the area's reputation for revelry. The glass facades are supported on a sheet-metal frame, and illuminated by LEDs at night. There are eateries at street level but the big draw is the eyrie Clouds (see p031). Also of note is the reopened Mojo Club (T 040 319 1999), a pioneer of the 1990s jazz-dance scene, which occupies splendid 9m-high basement vaults.
Reeperbahn 1

Chilehaus

Fritz Höger's behemoth is the most famous of Hamburg's unique *Kontorhäuser* (office buildings). It was constructed in 1924 for Henry B Sloman, an importer of nitrate from Chile, on two irregularly shaped plots. Höger's solution was a graciously pointed, 10-storey, ship-like landmark that became a symbol of Hamburg itself. Indeed, the daring shape inspired the logo of the city's 'Summer of Architecture' in 2003. Nearly five million red-and-violet-hued clinker bricks were utilised to create Höger's structure, which today houses private apartments and offices. Perhaps the most arresting feature is the courtyard and its archway entrances, which act as a symbolic gateway from the city's original merchants' quarter to the Speicherstadt (warehouse district). *Fischertwiete 2, www.chilehaus.de*

Flakturm IV

The monolithic Flakturm IV is one of the eight Flak Towers (anti-aircraft-gun blockhouses that also acted as shelters) commissioned by the Third Reich during WWII. Hitler's engineering team, the Organisation Todt, took bunker design to a new level and considered the buildings impenetrable (they were largely correct). Built in pairs (Flakturm IV's twin was later demolished), each tower provided a separate base for attack and command, with underground cables linking the two. About 18,000 people could take shelter behind the 3.5m-thick concrete walls of Flakturm IV, which had its own water and electricity supplies and hospital. Today, you will find recording studios and the popular live music venue Uebel & Gefährlich (www.uebelundgefaehrlich.com) inside. *Feldstrasse 66*

HOTELS

WHERE TO STAY AND WHICH ROOMS TO BOOK

It took a major sporting event to bring Hamburg's renaissance to wider attention. Since 2006, when the city hosted the FIFA World Cup, tourist numbers have grown annually. Hoteliers responded, and designers made their mark. Hip boutique hotel 25hours (Paul-Dessau-Strasse 2, T 855 070) sired a HafenCity offshoot (opposite); The George (see p022) brought style to the Aussenalster; David Chipperfield's Empire Riverside (Bernhard-Nocht-Strasse 97, T 311 190), a Miesian tower, has tremendous views; the funky Side (see p020) and East (see p023), and the venerable Atlantic Kempinski (An der Alster 72-79, T 28 880) all had an overhaul; and the 2014 arrival Henri (see p018) offers intimate retro charm.

Good value options include the YoHo (Moorkamp 5, T 284 1910) and York (Hofweg 19, T 227 1420), which have modern interiors within art nouveau buildings, and the quirky Superbude design hostels – the one on Juliusstrasse (No 1-7, T 807 915 820) boasts a Rockstar Suite with a stage/cinema. The Mövenpick (Sternschanze 6, T 334 4110), Gastwerk (Beim Alten Gaswerk 3, Daimlerstrasse, T 890 620) and Park Hyatt (Bugenhagenstrasse 8, T 3332 1234) are located in converted landmarks – a water tower, gasworks and *Kontorhaus* respectively. For longer stays, book a stylish apartment in the Wedina (Gurlittstrasse 23, T 280 8900) or the charming Von Deska Townhouses (Rothenbaumchaussee 197, T 180 390 210). *For full addresses and room rates, see Resources.*

25hours HafenCity

Architects Böge Lindner K2 and Stephen
Williams Associates, with designer Conni
Kotte, unfurled a full-on maritime look
for this 2011 hotel. The restaurant and
lobby are decked out with export crates
and flanked by freight containers used as
function rooms, and corridors are hung
with portraits of sea dogs. Hipsters hang
in the Club Floor, with its Macs, design
books, games and collection of Hamburg
vinyl. In the 170 rooms, such as L-Cabin 524
(above), the minibar and desk are inside
a steamer trunk, and wallpaper by Jindrich
Novotny is illustrated with sailors' tattoos.
The rooftop sauna has Elbe views. At the
original 25hours near Altona (see p016),
a lipstick-pink circular reception sets the
tone for the irreverent yet stylish interiors.
*Überseeallee 5, T 257 7770,
www.25hours-hotels.com/hafencity*

Henri Hotel

This immediately likeable boutique hotel was imaginatively inserted into a 1930s red-brick office block by architects Jan Klinker. Of the 65 rooms, the Loft Suites (No 603, opposite and above) on the top two floors, which also house a modest spa with a view, are decorated with authentic 1950s furniture (from sofas to writing bureaus and triangular tables), vintage telephones and wallpaper by local artist Katharina Haines. The cheery reception and lounge, a collaboration with Munich designer Marc-Ludolf von Schmarsow, has a wealth of retro touches, including an antique Triumph typewriter on which you are encouraged to leave feedback. But best of all, perhaps, is the location within striking distance of many city highlights. *Bugenhagenstrasse 21, T 554 3570, www.henri-hotel.com*

Side

Of all the city's design hotels, Side has the most arresting lobby. The soaring glass-and-stone atrium, courtesy of architects Jan Störmer, houses light installations by US artist Robert Wilson. Situated close to Jungfernstieg's smart shops, this is a party hotel with a clientele of intercontinental weekenders and media types. Designer Matteo Thun describes his interiors as 'Zen meets pop'. The rooms have a cream and beige scheme offset by pastel details, wood floors and quirks like square toilet seats. Thun's 'Supersassi' furniture litters the Sky Lounge (left) and the top-floor Flying Suites, which have kitchenettes and open-plan bathrooms. Other assets are the spa, sun terrace and (M)eatery (T 3099 9595) restaurant, which takes its steaks seriously, using a glass maturation booth and an infrared oven that reaches 800°C.
Drehbahn 49, T 309 990,
www.side-hamburg.de

The George

Hotelier Kai Hollmann's vision combines the elegance of a London members' club and the clarity of German design with a touch of Italian flair. Designer Sibylle von Heyden dressed the 125 rooms and suites in a rich colour palette, with chesterfield armchairs, Eames rocking chairs, chaises longues and escritoires, although all the Union Jacks are a bit overkill. The 58 sq m George Suite (above) has a separate living room and superb views. There's a lovely library with flock wallpaper and leather furniture overlooking a pretty garden; in-house restaurant DaCaio offers hearty Mediterranean cuisine as well as high tea in the bar (3pm-6pm); and the roof terrace, which has an adjoining spa (T 280 030 1814), is a popular meeting spot in summer.
Barcastrasse 3, T 280 0300,
www.thegeorge-hotel.de

East

Chicago-based architect Jordan Mozer has instilled his singular vision in an old iron foundry, creating a space that offers eye candy at every turn. In many of the 127 rooms, such as the XL Junior Suite (above), layout conventions are thrown out of the window – beds are placed in the middle of the floor, headboards shoot off at odd angles, tubs are freestanding and curves rule. Recycled aluminium and bronze elements have been specially cast in homage to the building's former function. The stunning in-house Yakshi's Bar, with its globular hanging teardrops, oversized organic-shaped furniture, giant bone-like structures set within the brick walls and salvaged birch and oak, make the hotel feel more like an urban club.
Simon-von-Utrecht-Strasse 31, T 309 930, www.east-hamburg.de

24 HOURS
SEE THE BEST OF THE CITY IN JUST ONE DAY

One element that you can't escape in Hamburg is water. Unlike the notoriously wet weather, its lakes, harbour and rivers are its pride and joy. The elegant Jungfernstieg by the Binnenalster has some lovely cafés in which to kickstart your day, or take the U-Bahn to Klippkroog (opposite) in up-and-coming Altona, before browsing the design stores at Stilwerk (see p072). For an art fix, take in an exhibition along the Kunstmeile (see p027) or make the trip south to the private Falckenberg Collection (Wilstorfer Strasse 71, Tor 2, T 3250 6762). Housed inside a tyre factory converted by Roger Bundschuh, it showcases site-specific works by John Bock, Gregor Schneider, Thomas Hirschhorn, Jonathan Meese and more.

If the sun is out, take a steamship tour with Alster-Touristik (Anleger Jungfernstieg, T 357 4240) or jump on a launch through the docks with Hadag (T 311 7070, www.hadag.de). Alternatively, traverse Mitte's bridges on foot to the red-brick Speicherstadt (warehouse quarter). This most architecturally coherent of the historic central districts, built from 1885 to 1912, is on the way to HafenCity (see p028), the progress of which can be seen in the big model at the InfoCenter. Head to Bistrot Vienna (see p030) for an early dinner (there's a no-bookings policy) before cocktails on the lake at A Mora (see p048), high up in Clouds (see p031) or, in summer, at beach club Strandperle (Övelgönne 60, T 880 1112). *For full addresses, see Resources.*

09.00 Klippkroog

This bistro is fully swathed in recycled oak, its inviting furniture designed by Wenzel Wittenburg. A century-old bathhouse, Klippkroog has kept its original plastered ceiling, below which hangs a bespoke lighting concept by Hamburg-based Marc Nelson, featuring a pulley system and scissor-style pendants from Ply (see p078). Whenever possible, organic ingredients are sourced from local farmers. Try the traditional northern-German breakfast of *Arme Ritter* (milk-soaked fried bread with apple compote and caramelised nuts) and take away a slice of the famous raspberry cheesecake. Shelves groan with homemade delights such as salad dressing, egg liqueur and jam. If you're here in the evening, try the *Crespelle* (small folded pancakes).
Grosse Bergstrasse 255, T 5724 4368,
www.klippkroog.de

10.30 Sleeping Dogs

This concept store offers a fine selection of brands from Hamburg and across Europe, displayed thoughtfully in a gallery-like warehouse that has a polished concrete floor and a layered-larchwood feature wall. Furniture and interior objects are artfully displayed and given space to breathe. On our visit we spied Montana's shelf modules (above); Studio Schneemann's lamps made out of recycled flip-flops; Jaime Hayón's porcelain figures for Lladró; Bocci's '28' series lights; Doshi Levien's 'My Beautiful Backside' sofa produced by Moroso; Ronan & Erwan Bouroullec's 'Losanges' rug for Nanimarquina; and a giant mural by local artist Cordula Ditz. Bimonthly 'exhibitions' often throw up gems, such as a collection of design classics by Piet Hein Eek. *Herrlichkeit 2, Rödingsmarkt 20, T 3861 4044, www.sleepingdogs.de*

11.30 Kunstmeile

The city's 'Art Mile' is impressive in scope. It encompasses the Kunsthalle (T 428 131 200), the largest gallery in the country outside Berlin, which features European works from the 1300s onwards and has a contemporary wing exhibiting art by the likes of Andreas Gursky and Olaf Metzel in the Galerie der Gegenwart. Smaller, avant-garde venues in the area are the Freie Akademie der Künste (T 324 632) and, in the same building, the Kunstverein (T 322 157). The Deichtorhallen (T 321 030) is set in a pair of converted hangar-like market halls, one of which hosts group art shows and the other photography with an interest in fashion, such as the work of East Germans Ute and Werner Mahler (above). Also in the building, the Fillet of Soul bistro (T 7070 5800) is a top choice for lunch, and from here it's a short hop to HafenCity.

15.00 HafenCity
The sheer magnitude of this waterfront development – not to mention its solid financial backing from both government and private enterprise – has attracted architects of the calibre of Herzog & de Meuron, David Chipperfield and Rem Koolhaas. Sandtorkai (pictured) was the first district to be completed, its colours evoking Speicherstadt over the canal.
InfoCenter, Sandtorkai 30, T 3690 1799

19.00 Bistrot Vienna

Dinner here is a memorable experience. Bistrot Vienna is located in a tiny space (it can only seat 32) on a residential street, and the wooden tables are so close together that communication with fellow diners is unavoidable (a summer terrace provides some breathing space). Forget counting calories and tuck into the creative cuisine, which often adds a twist to local dishes. Past highlights have included variations on the schnitzel, and pickled herrings with mango chutney, avocado and poppadoms. While you are eating dessert, chef/owner Sven Bunge will invariably pop out of the rear kitchen and strike up a conversation. Afterwards, take your coffee at the front bar, where locals enjoy a late-night natter.
Fettstrasse 2, T 439 9182, www.vienna-hamburg.de

21.30 Clouds

On the 23rd floor of Tanzende Türme (see p012), 105m up in the air, this restaurant provides the perfect Hamburg panorama. The European menu majors on steak and has a Gallic slant in hearty dishes such as seafood cassoulet and *tarte flambée*. The warm interior, designed by Florian Kienast, features oak tabletops, tan leather seating and bottle-laden shelves. There's a bar too, where it would be rude not to order a highball, although on warm nights head one floor up to the outdoor Heaven's Nest, glazed on all four sides. Here, you will find lounge furniture, sunbeds, a champagne bar, blissed-out sounds and unencumbered vistas. The venue attracts a broad mix of society, from after-workers to starry-eyed couples and the city's movers and shakers. *Reeperbahn 1, T 3099 3280, www.clouds-hamburg.de*

URBAN LIFE
CAFÉS, RESTAURANTS, BARS AND NIGHTCLUBS

Port cities usually produce colourful nightlife, and Hamburg is no exception. Combine a healthy alternative scene, an appreciation of design, a varied cuisine, a host of live-music venues and one of Europe's most infamous red-light districts, and you have a cocktail that's hard to beat. For a night of slumming it par excellence, the Reeperbahn still delivers. Everybody comes here, from designer-clad ad execs to kohl-painted goths. The main gig venue is Grosse Freiheit 36 (T 3177 7810), which puts on international acts, and the historic Moondoo (see p035) hosts a roster of club nights, yet there are countless watering holes along *die sündige Meile* (The Sinful Mile), such as the Golden Pudel Club (Fischmarkt 27, T 3197 9930).

Hamburg is rightly proud of its reputation for gastronomy, and it excels in terms of variety. Contemporary Italian is popular, as exemplified by LaBaracca (Sandtorkai 44, T 3006 1944) – where you order on a tablet PC – the much-lauded Anna Sgroi (see p042) and the slick but welcoming Cornelia Poletto (see p047). To sample indigenous food, you can't go wrong at Parlament (Rathausmarkt 1, T 7038 3399), set in the glorious Rathaus basement, Oberhafen-Kantine (Stockmeyerstrasse 39, T 3280 9984) and Bistrot Vienna (see p030). Tim Mälzer is Germany's Jamie Oliver and initially cut his teeth in the riverside Das Weisse Haus (Neumühlen 50, T 390 9016) before setting up the bold, buzzy Bullerei (see p052).
For full addresses, see Resources.

Idol Bar

The interior of this retro-chic watering hole is every bit as considered as its menu of craft beers and boutique whiskies and gins. Sibling owners Christoph and Martin Raub and designers We Are Visual recycled and upcycled a miscellany of found items. The bar is made from shipping containers, chairs were rescued from a school and lamps have been cut from propane gas cannisters, while the sculptures are by local artist Nils Knott. As well as six labels from Hamburg brewery Ratsherrn, Idol stocks a guest ale each week and bottles from other micro-producers, and also has a fine selection of premium spirits. The cultured music policy (jazz and 1930s and 1940s German swing) is pitched at just the right volume to allow for conversation. *Feldstrasse 37a, T 1805 2546, www.idolbar.de*

Nil

Elisabeth Füngers and Steffen Hellmann's restaurant has been deservedly popular for more than a quarter of a century. The curvaceous interior is classic Paris bistro: heavy red curtains and Gallic decorations. The various dining areas (which include a back garden) offer a surprising amount of intimacy thanks to the considered layout, especially on the first-floor mezzanine (above), where you'll find the best tables in the house. The predominantly French menu embraces contemporary German and Mediterranean influences and there's a laudable commitment to local, seasonal ingredients – perhaps try the wild garlic soup followed by cassoulet of Vierländer duck with bacon and mushrooms – and is accompanied by a well-curated wine list.
Neuer Pferdemarkt 5, T 439 7823, www.restaurant-nil.de

Moondoo

One of the Reeperbahn's buzziest clubs has a colourful history. As the Hippodrom, it became famous for topless rodeo shows (horses were kept in stables downstairs, now a second dancefloor) before Peter Eckhorn took over in the 1960s, renamed it Top Ten and hired a then-unknown group called The Beatles as the house band (they lived upstairs). In the mid-1990s it became dance club La Cage, and in 2007, Claus Hock transformed it into Moondoo with the help of local architects Raumschiff. The retro interior encompasses a table-service area (above) with art-deco-style pillars bedecked with gold leaf, luminous organic 'dance tables' and velvet seating, but the original Jugendstil tiling in the entrance is the most delightful surprise. *Reeperbahn 136, T 3197 5530, www.moondoo.de*

Henssler & Henssler

This spacious packing warehouse has been converted into a sleek restaurant by Werner Henssler and his son, Steffen, a celebrity chef who studied the art of sushi in LA and serves a creative take on Californian fusion. Book a table in the stylishly monochrome main space or on the terrace beside Dockland (see p010). *Grosse Elbstrasse 160, T 3869 9000, www.h2dine.de*

Tide

Chef Frank Walbeck combines both his passions – driftwood and food – at this serene café. When you arrive, Walbeck will often be preparing a bucketful of berries he has collected himself, which he then takes into his tiny back kitchen to slow cook and turn into jams. Beautifully bottled preserves, as well as olive oils and vinegars, are sold here, and all make great gifts to take home (the Tide Kit, a seasonal box containing cake, jam and sweets, is particularly fetching). You can also enjoy superior coffee, sandwiches and homemade cakes on the premises. When Walbeck is not working his magic in the kitchen, he is scouting deserted beaches in Denmark for driftwood, which he then sells as artwork – his pieces are dotted around the café and shop.
Rothestrasse 53, T 4111 1499, www.tide.dk

Kaffee Elbgold

Located in Schanzenhöfe, a redeveloped 19th-century industrial quarter that also encompasses Bullerei (see p052), Elbgold champions 'ethical coffee' sourced from fair-trade independent and cooperative producers in Africa, Indonesia and Latin America, such as Esmeralda Geisha from Panama. Within a former warehouse, much of the space is dedicated to the roasting process – two huge Probats are given star billing, and the main counter is dominated by a row of stylish black-steel silos from which beans are sold by the bag. A mixed crowd of suits and hipsters hang out in the sociable venue, sprawled on the 1960s chairs from Scandinavia, around the high table carved from a 250-year-old oak, or outside on the extensive terrace.
Lagerstrasse 34c, T 2351 7520,
www.elbgoldkaffee.de

20Up Skyline Bar

On a clear day or night, you can trace the Elbe's route to the ocean through the 9m-high windows of the 20th-floor bar at the Empire Riverside (see p016). The hotel, designed by David Chipperfield, opened in 2007 as part of a mixed-use rework of the Bavaria brewery. Its staggered volumes reflect the height of the surrounding eaves, although the tower, which has a glass-bronze facade, makes its own statement on the skyline. The long bar itself is made from acrylic bauxite and is topped by metal mesh, but all anyone is looking at are the views. At the weekend, dress up and make a reservation. Afterwards, follow those in the know to intimate club/DJ bar Ego (Talstrasse 9), or pile in a cab to the hip Le Lion (T 334 753 780; ring bell for entry). *Bernhard-Nocht-Strasse 97, T 311 190, www.empire-riverside.de*

Anna Sgroi

Firmly established on Hamburg's gastro scene, Milanese chef Anna Sgroi's latest venture is set in a restored 19th-century villa in well-heeled Pöseldorf. The building is divided into four areas: a reception with ornamental flagstones dominated by an apple-wood bar; a convivial main room with original stucco, hazelnut tables and a decorative Swedish oven; a more intimate carpeted room (above) that has art deco-style lamps by Olaf Thomas; and a terrace (opposite) shaded by a large, distinguished yew. Sgroi earned a Michelin star a few months after opening in 2013. The four- or five-course set menus feature impeccably presented Italian fusion – cod carpaccio, rabbit ravioli – and unusual ingredients such as sea urchin and stinging nettles. *Milchstrasse 7, T 2800 3930, www.annasgroi.de*

Die Bank

This 1897 bank, an exquisite example of
Jugendstil designed by Wilhelm Martens,
was converted into a restaurant in 2005.
The hall's interiors are the work of Herret
von Haeften of local firm Ramadeus, who
retained the chandeliers and the marble
pillars, and added leather furniture and
a 20m bar wrapped in gold and imprinted
with serial numbers. There is a walk-in
wine cabinet through the thick doors of
the old safe. Die Bank is a power-dining
destination, especially at lunch, when the
Veuve flows freely. Chef Thomas Fischer
won a Michelin star at Gogärtchen (T 46
514 1242), his venue in Sylt (see p096),
and specialises in fish and seafood again
here; we recommend the skate wings and
Matjes (herring) tartare. In summer, a grill
is set up on the terrace. Closed Sundays.
*Hohe Bleichen 17, T 0238 0030,
www.diebank-brasserie.de*

Café Paris

Reassuringly, this gorgeous monument to Jugendstil hasn't been overrun by tourists; locals are just as likely to be found sipping a pastis on the small terrace, which has a fine view of the Rathaus (see p009). It is difficult to believe that this 1882 building began life as a slaughterhouse. Now it is a stately European coffeehouse harking back to its glory days at the turn of the 20th century, and white-aproned waiters deliver French bistro staples from pâté to bouillabaisse and steak tartare. Settle into a banquette and, depending on the time of day, order the indulgent breakfast-for-two, a plate of macaroons or an oyster platter as you admire the exquisitely tiled art nouveau double-domed ceiling, which is illustrated with scenes of local industry. *Rathaustrasse 4, T 3252 7777, www.cafeparis.net*

Cornelia Poletto

After helming the Michelin-starred Poletto for a decade, TV chef Cornelia opened this less formal space in 2011, and is usually in the kitchen or greeting diners. Studio Jan Wichers gave the space a dark, elegant interior, all leather seating and black-and-white portraits of Monica Bellucci by Chico Bialas on the walls, as well as a communal table under two huge battered pendant lights. The menu is Italian with a twist, as is apparent in dishes like casarecce pasta served with game ragout and chanterelles. Alternatively, pick something up from the deli, which sells a fine range of homemade sauces, and try one of the 400 wines – we suggest the Schlossgut Diel Riesling from Nahe – in the company of the after-work crowd that gathers outside.
Eppendorfer Landstrasse 80, T 480 2159, www.cornelia-poletto.de

A Mora

Hamburg revels in its lakes. The smaller Binnenalster acts as a focal point and, thanks to development on Jungfernstieg, has plenty of terraces and benches from which to admire the Geneva-style fountain at its centre. The larger Aussenalster (it takes three hours to walk around) is more bucolic, and a millionaires' row skirts its shores. But you don't have to be one to enjoy the outdoor bars on the edge of the brilliant-blue water. You need to be quick, though, as on sunny days, beautiful locals head here in droves for a sunset cocktail. The place to be seen since 2006 is A Mora, a sleek, narrow bar on a jetty, all muted grey and cream, with daybeds arranged for prime views, a simple menu of salad, pasta and waffles, and sundown beats.
An der Alster, T 2805 6735,
www.a-mora.com

Weltbühne

The 'stage beyond the theatre' is how owner Tim Seidel describes Weltbühne, a throwback to a fin-de-siècle Weimar Republic *Kaffeehaus*, adjacent to the Thalia Theater. Hamburg-based Brit Stephen Williams' welcoming interior is a fine, contemporary interpretation of the 1920s, thanks to the Thonet furniture, cognac-coloured leather upholstery, art deco lighting, black-and-white tiled floor and a patchwork of portraits on the walls. From the kitchen comes a procession of French and German brasserie fare, as well as some Mediterranean dishes – the most popular choices are the steak frites and *Tafelspitz* (boiled beef in broth, Viennese-style). There's an excellent wine list too, which features plenty of German labels.
*Gerhart-Hauptmann-Platz 70,
T 3039 3250, www.weltbühne.net*

Hoch3

Meaning three floors, Hoch3 was the city's first late-night DJ bar, and was a welcome addition to the scene, considering many clubs don't open until 2am. It has a strong visual identity thanks to creative agency Weissraum, as well as a coherent industrial design featuring custom-made lacquered furniture, gold fabric-upholstered walls, darkwood panelling and a sleek concrete bar backed by an illuminated aquarium. Order a signature cocktail like the Crémant (Campari, Cointreau, sparkling wine and cranberry) or the own-recipe schnapps. From Thursdays to Saturdays, DJs mix party sounds under mirrored disco balls until 5.30am. Fuel up at the Pauline café and restaurant (T 4135 9964), which has a living-room vibe, in the courtyard below. *Neuer Pferdemarkt 4, T 7699 1881, www.hoch3.cc*

Bullerei
Chef-owners Tim Mälzer and Patrick Rüther converted an industrial shed into this hip deli/restaurant in 2009. Regional German cuisine is served in a cavernous space with peeling-plaster brick walls, lighting by Belgian company Dark and street-art murals by Elmar Lause. Musos occasionally perform under a solitary Poulsen light in the cosy back room.
Lagerstrasse 34b, T 3344 2110

INSIDER'S GUIDE

JOHANNA BRINCKMAN, PHOTOGRAPHER

Born and bred in the city, Johanna Brinckman travels for work but is always excited to return. 'Hamburg's creative and vibrant. I love this city. It has the perfect mix of urbanity and nature – the quality of life is so good.' On days off, she'll breakfast at Swedish-inspired Glück und Selig (Heussweg 97, T 3251 8975) and check out a show at Deichtorhallen (see p027) or the intimate Photography Monika Mohr Galerie (Mittelweg 45, T 4135 0350): 'I've been going there since I was little.' She recommends Stilwerk (see p072) as a 'must for design' and, for relaxation, the rooftop spa at The George (see p022). However, if the sun is out, she'll cycle over to the beach on the river in Elbstrand and later retire to the terrace at Zum Bäcker (Strandweg 65, T 864 800): 'The perfect spot for a sunset dinner.'

Brinckman takes visitors to Henssler & Henssler (see p036) and then on to IndoChine (Neumühlen 11, T 3980 7880) in summer to party by the water. With friends, she either grabs a gourmet burger from Dulf's (Himmelstrasse 45, T 4600 7633) or books a table at Bullerei (see p052) before heading west to Clockers (Paul-Roosen-Strasse 27, T 176 7249 3595), where she cosies up in an armchair with a whisky and soda. If it's going to be a big night, she'll catch a gig in Terrace Hill (Medienbunker Heiligengeistfeld, Feldstrasse 66, T 7296 4440) or make a beeline for Off Club (Leverkusenstrasse 54, T 8901 9333) for its 'creative interior and super-cool vibe'.
For full addresses, see Resources.

ARCHITOUR
A GUIDE TO HAMBURG'S ICONIC BUILDINGS

Hamburg's allure lies in its contrasts. The future is HafenCity (see p028), which aspires to be a 'city within a city'. The first residents moved into Sandtorkai in 2009, and more than two million sq m of floor space is planned. The light shows at the stations on the new U4 metro line are striking examples of the design ethic.

Although Hamburg suffered widespread bomb damage during WWII, the clinker-brick tradition lasted longer in north Germany than in the rest of the country, and the best examples, such as the Chilehaus (see p013), can be seen in the Kontorhausviertel (office district). Art nouveau buildings fared less well, although there are pockets of Jugendstil in Mitte and, more coherently, in Eppendorf.

Now, local firm Bothe Richter Teherani (BRT) is a key presence (see p062). Other German studios heavily involved include Berlin's J Mayer H (see p060) and Behnisch from Stuttgart (see p067), who devised the Chamber of Commerce's Haus im Haus, a clever extension within the original neoclassical pile (Adolphsplatz 1). Most fascinating are the 70 projects of the International Building Exhibition (IBA), held from 2006 to 2013 on Wilhelmsburg island, championing sustainability and innovation. Tours (T 226 227 228, www.iba-hamburg.de) cover the likes of the Energiebunker (see p058) and BIQ housing block (Inselpark 17), which has microalgae in its glass facade that photosynthesise solar energy into heat. *For full addresses, see Resources.*

Congress Center

This radical masterpiece by Jost Schramm and Gerd Pempelfort was some 10 years in development, but with the help of town planner Ernst May, Germany's very first congress centre opened in 1973 with the then Plaza Hotel towering over it. Already one of the largest conference venues in Europe, it was expanded with a massive glass-and-steel extension, designed by architects K2B, on the perimeter of the Planten un Blomen botanical gardens. The hotel, which is still the highest in town, is now a Radisson Blu. A renovation in 2011 by Swedish interior designer Christian Lundwall gave its 556 rooms a sleek look. The High End event space (T 35 020) on the 26th and 27th floors has giddy views over Hamburg and is often open to the public – it's best to call ahead to check. *Marseiller Strasse 1, T 35 690, www.cch.de*

Energiebunker
Architects HHS used galvanised steel to transform this hulking flak tower into a renewable-power station in 2013. A heat reservoir supplied by solar panels, waste energy and wood-chip and biomethane generators powers 3,000 homes. Up top, VJU Café (Wednesday to Sunday, until 6pm) has an interior by Ply (see p078) and a 30m-high cantilevered terrace.
Neuhöfer Strasse 7, T 0152 3373 8337

ADA 1

Completed in 2009, ADA 1 quickly earned an assured place on the Aussenalster lake. It was designed by Berlin-based architects J Mayer H, whose skilled combination of technology and creativity has garnered a string of awards. The six-storey office sits between dense downtown and the water, its sinuous curves complementing the park that fronts it. Distinctive oval windows (dubbed 'floating eyes') house meeting rooms and provide natural light. More of J Mayer H's highly distinctive work can be seen to the north of HafenCity, where an almost impossibly dimensioned block, S11 (Steckelhörn 11), is squeezed between two historic structures. The firm has also left its signature with the 2012 Schlump ONE (Schäferkampsallee 16-18), a voluptuous revamp of a 1950s building in Eimsbüttel.
An der Alster 1

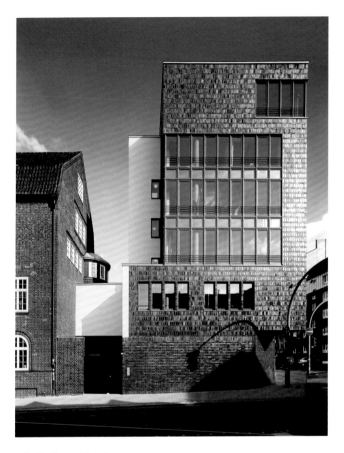

Polizeirevier Davidwache

This well-loved Hamburg landmark was designed by Fritz Schumacher, the city planner and co-founder of the Deutscher Werkbund group, an alliance of architects and craftsmen who advocated a mix of industrial and artisanal methods. The police station has reigned over Hamburg's den of iniquity, the Reeperbahn, since 1914, and even became the subject of a 1964 film by Jürgen Roland. In 2003-2004, architect Bernhard Winking added an extension to the rear, a cubic structure (above) that alludes to Schumacher's prewar Hamburg – he acted as chief town planning officer from 1909 to 1933, lending the city its clinker-brick character. The extension adds large windows and a top storey, giving the policemen a better viewpoint over their rowdy precinct.
Spielbudenplatz 31

Elbberg Campus

Local studio BRT has no less than three major works between the Elbe and the Altonaer Balkon. Located near Dockland (see p010) and encompassing the Habitat store (Grosse Elbstrasse 264), which is shaped like a container ship and has an expansive wooden roof terrace, Elbberg Campus is a modular, open-plan complex of lofts and workspaces. Situated at the base of a grassy cliff, it overlooks the harbour warehouses. The exteriors match their surroundings – on the south side a glass facade reflects light and the water, whereas the land-facing north aspect is clad in copper. BRT have crammed four storeys into a difficult wedge-shaped site, connecting the buildings via landscaped stairs and walkways, which create a self-contained meeting point on the hillside.
Elbberg 6-8, www.elbbergcampusaltona.de

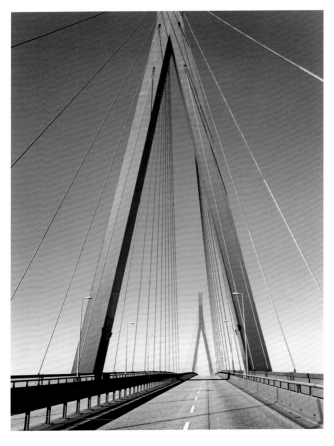

Köhlbrandbrücke

To see this marvel of concrete engineering up close, you'll need a car or a water taxi because the 1974 Köhlbrandbrücke is only open to pedestrians on special occasions. Designed by the architects Hans Wittfoht and Egon Jux, it crosses the south branch of the Elbe on the way to HafenCity; you may well pass over it in a cab on the drive in from the airport. In a city of some 2,500 bridges, this is the largest by far – 12,700 tonnes of steel form its 75 pylons and 88 cables. And at almost 4km long and 55m high, the Köhlbrandbrücke is a soaring example of cable-stayed design that has become a symbol of the modern city, its broad, high sweep appearing on postage stamps and providing an iconic route for the UCI World Tour Vattenfall Cyclassics bike race at the end of August.
A7 Autobahn, Waltershof

Floating Homes

It wasn't until 2006 that city authorities granted permission for the development of housing on the water, and one of the first settlements was in the Hochwasserbassin (pictured). The attractive dwellings, made from wood, steel and glass, have heated floors, skydecks and adaptable interior walls, and add-ons like photovoltaic cells (they're not cheap, though). In addition to the bucolic surroundings, the Floating Homes have as a backdrop BRT's Berliner Bogen Office (Anckelmannsplatz 1), which was built over the canal in 2001. The steel-and-glass landmark lies on the rail route from Berlin, making it a dramatic first glimpse of Hamburg's forward-thinking architecture. Parabolic steel trusses carry the load of the vault-like structure, and interior gardens harness solar energy.
T 042 1277 4050, www.floatinghomes.de

Dock 47

Vivid, asymmetrical Dock 47 springs out of the flat St Pauli landscape like a flame. This dynamic office building, with its deep-red panels and outward-leaning walls on two sides, was conceived by local practice Spengler Wiescholek. Completed in 2004, the beacon stands on a sloping site at a hectic traffic intersection opposite the 300-year-old Fischmarkt – the interplay between the two is a striking metaphor for new and old Hamburg. Dock 47 is the standout achievement in a cluster that includes another Spengler Wiescholek project, Pinnasberg 45. Despite its more conventional shape, the 2005 office block leaves an impression via its aquamarine facade of ivy-patterned enamelled glass. It's a short walk from the Reeperbahn and the Polizeirevier Davidwache (see p061). *Pinnasberg 47, www.dock47.de*

Unilever HQ and Marco Polo Tower

Architects Behnisch's ensemble justifies its prime Elbe location. Unilever (Strandkai 1) is the larger trapezoidal volume (above left), wrapped in a protective second skin that enables airflow through operable interior windows. The environmentally friendly edifice uses a third of the energy of the previous HQ and won Best Office Building at the 2009 World Architecture Awards. Its public atrium contains a mall and spa and is crisscrossed by bridges and ramps that mirror the cityscape. Adjacent to Unilever is the 2010 Marco Polo Tower (Hübenerstrasse), composed of 17 storeys, each turned a few degrees on its axis to maximise views. Features recur yet no floor replicates another, resulting in a twisting 55m spiral with organic curves. The complex sits among the gardens and concrete landscaping of Kaipromenade.

Staatsoper

Hamburg's opera house dates back more than 300 years (its first incarnation was a shed-like affair) and has been graced by Gustav Mahler and Richard Wagner – it hosted its first complete *Ring Cycle* in 1879. Distel and Grubitz's art deco building, the basic structure of which you see today, was completed in 1926, but its auditorium was destroyed during WWII. The Bauhaus architect Gerhard Weber rebuilt it in 1955,

and a concrete-and-glass extension was added by Kleffel Köhnholdt und Partner in 2005. The 8,500 sq m interior comprises three stages, offices and workshops for costumiers and make-up artists, and is home to the State Opera, the Ballet and the Philharmonic, until the latter joins the migration to HafenCity (see p071) in 2017. *Grosse Theaterstrasse 25, T 356 868, www.hamburgische-staatsoper.de*

Spiegel HQ

The German media group relocated to the north tip of HafenCity in 2011, its flagship designed by Danish architects Henning Larsen. The angular glass box's recessed facade symbolises either a 'window to the city' or a giant TV, depending on whether you prefer the official or local viewpoint. Its 14 floors rest on a red-tiled foundation that references nearby Speicherstadt, and, like many other new offices in the area, it is highly efficient. A 61m atrium facilitates natural ventilation, the temperature is regulated by geothermal energy via 320 underground pipes, and the building does not need AC or heating systems. In a nod to Spiegel's heritage, the canteen references Verner Panton's 1969 original, now moved lock, stock and barrel to the Museum für Kunst und Gewerbe (T 428 134 880).
Ericusspitze 1, Brooktorkai

Elbphilharmonie

Disputes over the cost (€865m and rising) have delayed inauguration of this concert hall until 2017, a decade after the first stone was laid. But even part-finished in 2014, the Elbphilharmonie was fulfilling its role as a landmark of civic pride, a shining beacon at the harbour entrance. Designed by Herzog & de Meuron, its unusual semi-translucent glass facade incorporates gill-like openings and fish-mouth balconies, the roof rearing up like storm waves to a height of 110m. It is seemingly plonked on a 1966 brick warehouse, yet the structure is well integrated. The auditorium, a bubble decoupled from the rest of the building to aid soundproofing, seats 2,100 around a central stage. The complex will also house recital halls, a hotel and 45 apartments. *Kaiserkai, T 3576 6666,* *www.elbphilharmonie.de*

SHOPPING
THE BEST RETAIL THERAPY AND WHAT TO BUY

As soon as you arrive in Hamburg, you will realise its inhabitants love to shop. There are more department stores here than in any other German city, the best of which is Alsterhaus (Jungfernstieg 16-20, T 359 010). The 'shopping mile' comprises pedestrianised Spitalerstrasse, upmarket Jungfernstieg and Mönckebergstrasse. At Neuer Wall, you will find big guns such as local fashion maven Jil Sander (No 43, T 374 1290), and at Hohe Bleichen you'll come across Petra Teufel (No 13, T 3786 1610), which stocks the likes of Lala Berlin and Isabel Marant. In upscale, residential Eppendorf, the many eclectic boutiques include stylist Conni Kotte (Bismarck Strasse 103, T 8079 0224), who gathers vintage and modern design in her gallery of creative ideas, and Kaufrausch (Isestrasse 74, T 480 8313), which is the city's answer to Colette.

Although a touch gritty, the Schanze area throws up some real retail treasures, such as the emporium of fashion designer Anna Fuchs (see p082). Elsewhere, Kunst und Gemüse (Wexstrasse 28, T 4328 0772) sells recycled glassware, while for more fashion and interior design visit Stilwerk (Grosse Elbstrasse 68, T 3062 1100), a mall of cutting-edge shops located in a converted malt factory. North of here is Ply (see p078), always one of the first places we head to when back in town, for its beautifully restored midcentury furniture, as well as The Box (see p080), which ticks them all. *For full addresses, see Resources.*

Mutterland

Launched by designer and restaurateur Jan Schawe, who founded A Mora (see p048), Mutterland's motto is 'Made in Germany'. It sells enticingly packaged delicacies produced by more than 200 farmers and family-run businesses, such as slow-food jams from Freche Früchtchen, fruit spirits, chocolate from Kakao Kontor and more unusual items such as FC St Pauli ketchup. The Monkey 47 Schwarzwald Dry Gin from the Black Forest (above), €39.80 for 500ml, is made from 47 ingredients that include spruce sprouts, cranberry, elderberry, sloe, blackberry and spices. Mutterland's three branches in Hamburg all have a country-kitchen vibe; the one in Ernst-Merck-Strasse (T 2840 7978) has a café where homemade soups, pies and more are served until 9pm (7pm on Sundays). *www.mutterland.de*

Koppel 66
This renovated arcade is Hamburg's hub for arts and crafts. Highlights include the elegant wood-turned fountain pens of Stefan Fink, produced in his workshop (pictured; T 247 151), unique hats from milliner Teresa Gaschler (T 4850 9235) and handcrafted men's brogues by Annabelle Stephan (T 248 010). Refuel at the courtyard Café Koppel (T 249 235).
Koppel 66, T 3864 1930

Wohnkultur 66

Set in the former slaughterhouse district, this furniture warehouse specialises in 20th-century Scandinavian design. Its raison d'être is one man, the late Danish master craftsman Finn Juhl. Owners Martina Münch and Manfred Werner, who describe discovering Juhl's work as a life-altering experience, are the sole distributors of his furniture in Germany and one of only a handful of authorised distributors worldwide. The pieces are still made to exacting standards and production is extremely limited. Prices reflect this, but as Juhl's more iconic items, such as the 'Pelican' chair, have reached five figures at auction, they make a solid investment. Wohnkultur 66 now also stocks pieces by another Danish company, Brdr Petersen. *Sternstrasse 66, T 436 002, www.wohnkultur66.de*

Dorothea Schlueter

After a decade as the artist-run Trottoir, which occupied one shop window in the Portuguese quarter, this gallery, named after the mythical Dorothea Schlueter, now resides in a former office in an elegant Wilhelminian building with original stucco detailing and parquet floors. The focus is on upcoming German ('Du' paintings by Berlin artist Rocco Pagel, above) and international talent, with an emphasis on experimental work and installations. On opening nights every six weeks or so, you can mingle with the curators and artists in the shocking-yellow kitchenette designed by Mexico City architects Pedro & Juana. The gallery also runs a publishing house, Textem, which produces books, catalogues and the magazine *Kultur & Gespenster*. *Grosse Bäckerstrasse 4, T 3197 3763, www.dorotheaschlueter.com*

Ply

Displayed in this former fish smokehouse is an awe-inspiring selection of industrial design, lamps and decorative items from the 1920s to the 1960s, from pharmacy filing cabinets to Eames office chairs, neon signage and furniture by Egon Eiermann. The owners also use a 1950s Korrex press and wood type to create limited-edition art prints. Open 12pm to 6pm; closed Sundays. *Hohenesch 68, T 3866 1020, www.ply.de*

The Box

Within a listed building in the redeveloped Borselhof factory complex, this unmissable showroom, dominated by a chandelier by local Florian Borkenhagen, is full of highly desirable and unusual creations that catch the eye, from drum kits to vintage bikes, Ralph Lauren lamps, George Smith sofas and Tom Dixon tableware. A separate room is stacked with high-end kitchen products, and a café/bar hosts readings, gigs and events. The buzzy venue also incorporates a bookstore and a pair of galleries: The Box sells art, sculpture and photography by the likes of Peter Beard, as well as vintage furniture; and Lazy Dog (T 151 2263 3399), the city's first design gallery, has a fine pan-European portfolio encompassing work by Oskar Zieta and Susanna Hertrich. *Borselstrasse 16f, T 3990 6214, www.thebox-hamburg.com*

Anna Fuchs
Poised on the edge of greatness, fashion designer Anna Fuchs is big on dresses reminiscent of 1940s styles – belted, nipped and flowing creations in crêpe and silk jersey – and coats that evoke the golden age of Dior. Her recent collections have featured knitwear, stylish jumpsuits and unconventional suits.
Karolinenstrasse 27, T 4018 5408, www.annafuchs.de

D'Or

On a chichi strip of Eppendorf's high street, this novel shop has four distinct sections, each with different owners. At the front is a jeweller that carries designs by Sabine Klarner, Marion Becker, Annette Albrecht and Natalie von Matt. The rear of the store houses Tobias Scholl's art deco and 20th-century antiques (above; T 4688 1974), from Belgian ceramics to French porcelain and paste jewellery. Scholl stocks his own 1930s-inspired mirrored furniture too, as well as modern work from Raynaud and Claus Porto. D'Or also has a zone devoted to vintage designer fashion – head here for a classic Jil Sander blazer (hard to find since the label was bought out by Prada); as well as a concession (T 4688 1881) of department store Petra Teufel (see p072). *Eppendorfer Baum 6, T 4688 1963, www.d-or.de*

Roomservice

Artist Julia Thesenfitz and architect Christian Wedekind opened their high-end interiors store in a Jugendstil house in one of Eppendorf's prettiest streets in 2002. The remit is broad and the couple are as dedicated to giving exposure to emerging talent – such as Central Saint Martins alumnus Elisa Strozyk, who makes wood-veneer 'textiles' in the shape of rugs, wallpaper, lampshades and even dresses – as to more established players. Classics on display (above) during our visit included the 'Raimond Zafu' pendant light by Raimond Puts for Moooi and the 'Taccia' table light by Achille Castiglioni for Flos, but we were most taken by the 'Pluma Cubic' goose-feather lampshade by Berlin designer Heike Buchfelder. *Lehmweg 56, T 480 8672, www.roomservice-gallery.com*

Lys Vintage

Hamburg is a short hop from Scandinavia, and Lys (meaning light) brings it even closer with a gorgeous collection of vintage furniture and reissues from the 1950s and 1960s. There might be lamps by Poul Henningsen or Verner Panton, or Kay Bojesen's wooden animals, as well as choice classics by non-Scandis, including Jean-Louis Domecq's 'Signal' desk lamps. Displayed alongside are contemporary pieces from northern European producers including Hay, Secto Design, Zweed and Gubi. All is organised mise en scène in an art-gallery-like space, with wallpaper by the UK's Cole & Son or Danish firm Ferm Living in statement blocks. We liked Jenny Bäck's 1950s-inspired 'Lean' floor lamp, €289, and an oak sideboard, €1,790, designed by Gesa Hansen (both right).
Eppendorfer Weg 8, T 6966 2795, www.lys-vintage.com

SPORTS AND SPAS

WORK OUT, CHILL OUT OR JUST WATCH

Active pursuits in Hamburg are not hard to come by, owing to the abundance of water and green space. Running is popular, and each morning hundreds of locals don their Nikes to jog 7.5km around the Aussenalster lake. If time is tight, Touristjogging (T 439 8780, www.touristjogging.de) organises on-the-run tours of the city's main sights. For a sophisticated swim, visit Alster-Schwimmhalle (Ifflandstrasse 21, T 188 890), a dramatic 1973 building by Walter Neuhäusser. On a summer's day, head over to the pier/café Bodo's Bootssteg (Harvestehuder Weg 1b) to mess about in boats on the lake or to sunbathe in deckchairs while supping on a refreshing *Alsterwasser* (beer and sprite). Or watch Hamburg's lauded polo team in action from their 1928 Bauhaus clubhouse (Jenischstrasse 26, T 820 681), a labour of love for architect Heinrich Amsinck.

Hamburg is the home of Nivea, and Nivea Haus (Jungfernstieg 51, T 8222 4740) offers massages, facials and treatments. Superior hotel spas include the colourful retreat at Side (see p020) and the indoor/outdoor Mandarin Body & Soul (T 3099 3205) at East (see p023). Power Yoga Germany (T 3863 2264) has drop-in classes at stylish branches in Winterhude (Herderstrasse 38) and Schanze (Ludwigstrasse 10), but the most aesthetically pleasing workout is to be had at Y8 (see p092). For an old-school scrub-down, sample the Turkish delight Das Hamam (Feldstrasse 39, T 4135 9112). *For full addresses, see Resources.*

Aspria Spa

Situated near Aussenalster lake in leafy Uhlenhorst, this comprehensive hotel spa and sports club is set in extensive gardens. The boxy construction by architects SWP modishly incorporates wood, brick, stone, concrete, glass and tiles, and is matched to an 'English club' interior – chesterfields, panelled desks, fireplaces – by London's Sparcstudio. Visit in summer as, in addition to all the state-of-the-art treatments and facilities, there's an alfresco 20m lap pool, external saunas, landscaped terraces and an infinity whirlpool that connects inside and out. Alternatively, the Park Hyatt (see p016) offers day passes (€35) for its Club Olympus spa (T 3332 1736), which has a mosaicked indoor pool. Its massages and beauty therapies are deservedly popular. *Hofweg 40, T 5201 9010, www.aspria-alstertal.de*

Imtech Arena

The 1953 home ground of Bundesliga team Hamburger SV was revamped by architects MOS to turn it into one of the 12 host stadiums for the Germany World Cup. It's distinctive for its spoked-wheel membrane roof, designed by Stuttgart firm Schlaich Bergermann und Partner, which is supported by 40 exterior steel masts. The arena seats 57,274 and is also used for concerts. Slightly morbidly, Hamburger supporters can choose to be buried nearby, under turf from the original pitch. The devotion is equally strong at rivals FC St Pauli, whose *Kult* fans are known for their social activism, left-wing politics, punk attitude and skull-and-crossbones insignia. Their Millerntor ground is next to Flakturm IV (see p014). *Sylvesterallee 7, Volkspark, T 018 0547 8478, www.imtech-arena.de*

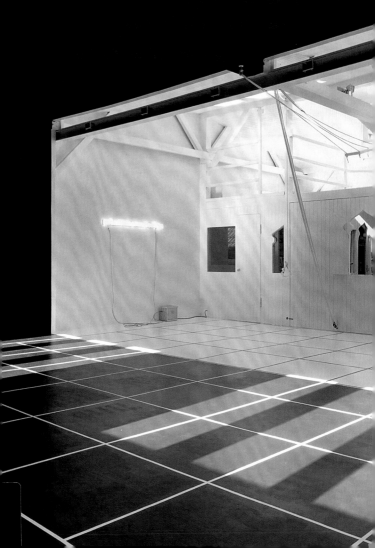

Y8 Yoga Studio

Artists Benita and Immanuel Grosser's Y8 is surely one of Europe's most inspiring yoga spaces. The main room, built from inexpensive plywood and painted white, is informed by Vastu Shastra architecture, which is based on the theory of space as a dynamic element from which everything comes into existence – and ultimately disappears. The Mandala grid comprises an astrologically calculated 64 squares of 94cm by 94cm that translates into 32 stations, upon which mats face east. The studio displays site-specific work by well-known conceptual artists such as Katharina Grosse, Carl Andre, Klaus Frahm, Joseph Kosuth (*Five Words in White Neon*, opposite) and Channa Horwitz (*Displacement*, above). It is run on a voluntary, non-profit basis.
Kleiner Kielort 8, T 4142 4546, www.artyoga.de

Golf Lounge

Located beside a canal (where else?) to the east of HafenCity, the three-level Golf Lounge has a series of putting greens and a driving range with 40 covered practice bays, which are attractively lit up at night (above). A rechargeable card allows you to hit up to 800 balls. Lessons are also available here, and there's a nine-hole fun course for those who don't take their swing quite so seriously. The stylish bar and coffee lounge, which has black-resin wicker garden furniture and views across the fairway, does a fine line in cocktails, chillout music and boutique burgers. Alternatively, visit one of the city's many courses, such as the pay-and-play Red Golf Hamburg-Moorfleet (T 788 7720), which has an attractive wood clubhouse. *Billwerder Neuer Deich 40, T 8197 8790, www.golflounge.info*

ESCAPES

WHERE TO GO IF YOU WANT TO LEAVE TOWN

Autobahns with no speed limits and a very efficient train system enhance the pleasure of jaunts out of Hamburg. The high-velocity ICE train whisks you off to Berlin in about 90 minutes, while more bucolic pursuits can be found in the outlying villages and towns. Blankenese (which can be reached on the S-Bahn) is the region's most picturesque village, situated on a hill overlooking the Elbe.

Less than an hour away by train, Lübeck still conjures up some of the splendour it enjoyed as the capital of the Hanseatic League. Two of its institutions are dedicated to giants of German culture: the Günter Grass-Haus (Glockengiesserstrasse 21, T 045 1122 4230), which shows the writer's early work as a sculptor and painter; and the baroque Buddenbrookhaus (Mengstrasse 4, T 045 1122 4190), Heinrich and Thomas Mann's family home. Stop for lunch in the medieval dining room of the Schiffergesellschaft (Breite Strasse 2, T 045 176 770), which charmingly translates as 'guild of the blue water captains'. An hour further east along the coast is Germany's first spa town, Heiligendamm, and the brick Gothic maritime city of Rostock, the jumping-off point for the boat to Rügen (see p100).

Sylt, known as the 'Hamptons of Germany', is the most famous of the North Sea Islands, and is a three and a half hour journey. Once a refuge for poets and painters, it attracts the jet set with its pristine (often nudist) beaches, thatched cottages and boutiques. *For full addresses, see Resources.*

Müritzeum, Waren

Two and a half hours' drive to the east, this ecology centre is located in the medieval town of Waren on the edge of the largest lake in Germany, Müritz, a lovely sight in spring when thousands of cranes migrate there. Swedish architects Wingårdhs have blended the building into the landscape beautifully. It appears to float as if it were moored, its facade clad with charcoaled larch, echoing the regional vernacular.

Müritzeum champions the flora and fauna of the Mecklenburger Seenplatte (known as the 'land of a thousand lakes'), shown in a series of multimedia and interactive exhibitions. It also houses the country's largest freshwater aquarium, in which whole shoals of fish are visible through a giant glass screen that spans two floors. *Zur Steinmole 1, T 039 9163 3680, www.mueritzeum.de*

Houseboats, Hvide Sande, Denmark
Denmark's proximity to north Germany
makes it a popular escape, and these
simple yet stylish houseboats are little
more than a three-hour car journey from
Hamburg. Anchored on the Ringkøbing
Fjord, a magnificent wetland and bird
sanctuary in the West Jutland district,
the five floating homes, which can sleep
between five and eight, were designed
by Aarhus-based firm Cubo Arkitekter.
Each lower deck holds a kitchen/family
room, one or two double bedrooms and
a pair of verandas. On the upper deck,
the living room overlooks the fjord, and
there's another veranda with space for
a barbecue. Cubo has also designed nine
houseboats at Bork Havn (T +45 7528
0344), further south on the same fjord.
*Tyskerhavn, T +45 9659 3593,
www.nordsee.dk*

Cerês Hotel, Binz, Rügen
Dubbed the 'Capri of the North', Rügen is an island of beech forests, chalk cliffs and sandy beaches. The town of Binz is renowned for its *Bäderarchitektur*: whitewashed early 20th-century villas with playful Jugendstil elements, including verandas with ornamental wood carvings, pinnacles and towers. Slotting serenely into this picturesque scene is Cerês Hotel, designed by Moritz Lau-Engehausen, in which minimal-chic rooms (Sea Deluxe Grand 313, above) come with bathtubs of Corian or black sandstone, and many have balconies overlooking the water; the Cupola Suite 301 (opposite) has stunning night views of the starry sky. Settle into a *Strandkorb* (roofed wicker chair) on the beach or chill out in the Senso Spa. It's a two-hour drive from Hamburg to Rostock, from where ferries depart in summer.
Strandpromenade 24, T 038 3936 6670, www.ceres-hotel.de

Weserburg, Bremen

Part of a clutch of former warehouses on a peninsula in the River Weser, Bremen's modern art museum has a location to match its singular approach. Opened in 1991, it displays select works from private European collections, among them the pictorial/sculptural art of the Finkenberg Collection; Siegfried Loch's assemblage of paintings themed around the colour blue; and 'Double Rotation Works' (pictured), one of the Lafrenz Collection's conceptual installations. The building itself was a tobacco factory in the early 1900s and is a stroll from Bremen's historic centre, 120km south-west of Hamburg. Closed Mondays. Stay in the stylish ÜberFluss hotel (T 042 132 2860), designed by Dutch firm Concrete. *Teerhof 20, T 042 159 8390, www.weserburg.de*

NOTES

SKETCHES AND MEMOS

RESOURCES

CITY GUIDE DIRECTORY

HOTELS
ADDRESSES AND ROOM RATES

Atlantic Kempinski 016
Room rates:
double, from €210
An der Alster 72-79
T 28 880
www.kempinski.com

Bork Havn Houseboats 099
Room rates:
Houseboat, from €480 per week
Kirkehøjvej 17
Bork Havn
Denmark
T +45 7528 0344
www.nordsee.dk

Cerês Hotel 100
Room rates:
double, from €180;
Sea Deluxe Grand 313, €220;
Glass Cupola Suite 301, €580
Strandpromenade 24
Binz
Rügen
T 038 3936 6670
www.ceres-hotel.de

East 023
Room rates:
double, from €155;
XL Junior Suite, €240
Simon-von-Utrecht-Strasse 31
T 309 930
www.east-hamburg.de

Empire Riverside 016
Room rates:
double, €130
Bernhard-Nocht-Strasse 97
T 311 190
www.empire-riverside.de

Gastwerk Hotel 016
Room rates:
double, from €140
Beim Alten Gaswerk 3
Daimlerstrasse
T 890 620
www.gastwerk.com

The George 022
Room rates:
double, from €155;
The George Suite, €325
Barcastrasse 3
T 280 0300
www.thegeorge-hotel.de

Henri Hotel 018
Room rates:
double, from €140;
Loft Suite, from €160;
Loft Suite 603, from €180
Bugenhagenstrasse 21
T 554 3570
www.henri-hotel.com

Hvide Sande Houseboats 098
Room rates:
Houseboat, from €400 per week
Tyskerhaven
Hvide Sande
Denmark
T +45 9659 3593
www.nordsee.dk

Mövenpick Hotel 016
Room rates:
double, from €150
Sternschanze 6
T 334 4110
www.wasserturm-schanzenpark.de

Park Hyatt 016
Room rates:
double, from €210
Bugenhagenstrasse 8
T 3332 1234
www.hamburg.park.hyatt.com

Side 020
Room rates:
double, from €160;
Flying Suite, €325
Drehbahn 49
T 309 990
www.side-hamburg.de

Superbude St Pauli 016
Room rates:
double, from €60;
Rockstar Suite, from €200
Juliusstrasse 1-7
T 807 915 820
www.superbude.de

25hours 016
Room rates:
double, from €95
Paul-Dessau-Strasse 2
T 855 070
www.25hours-hotels.com

25hours HafenCity 017
Room rates:
double, €120;
L-Cabin 524, €140
Überseeallee 5
T 257 7770
www.25hours-hotels.com/hafencity

ÜberFluss Hotel 103
Room rates:
double, from €170
Langenstrasse 7
Bremen
T 042 132 2860
www.hotel-ueberfluss.de

Von Deska Townhouses 016
Room rates:
double, from €140
The White House
Rothenbaumchaussee 197
T 180 390 210
www.vondeska-townhouses.de

Hotel Wedina 016
Room rates:
double, from €125
Gurlittstrasse 23
T 280 8900
www.wedina.de

YoHo 016
Room rates:
double, from €120
Moorkamp 5
T 284 1910
www.yoho-hamburg.de

Hotel York 016
Room rates:
one-bedroom apartment, from €115
Hofweg 19
T 227 1420
www.hotel-york.de

WALLPAPER* CITY GUIDES

Executive Editor
Rachael Moloney

Editor
Jeremy Case

Authors
Paul Sullivan
Camilla Péus

Art Editor
Eriko Shimazaki
Original Design
Loran Stosskopf
Map Illustrator
Russell Bell

Photography Editor
Elisa Merlo
**Assistant Photography
Editor**
Nabil Butt

Production Manager
Vanessa Todd-Holmes

Chief Sub-Editor
Nick Mee

Editorial Assistant
Emilee Jane Tombs

Contributors
Tina Engler
Karin Mecklenburg
Suzanne Wales

Interns
Blossom Green
Ayaka Nakamura

Wallpaper* ® is a
registered trademark
of IPC Media Limited

First published 2008
Revised and updated
2012 and 2014

© Phaidon Press Limited

All prices are correct at
the time of going to press,
but are subject to change.

Printed in China

Phaidon Press Limited
Regent's Wharf
All Saints Street
London N1 9PA

Phaidon Press Inc
65 Bleecker Street
New York, NY 10012

Phaidon® is a registered
trademark of Phaidon
Press Limited

www.phaidon.com

A CIP Catalogue record for
this book is available from
the British Library.

ISBN 978 0 7148 6826 4

PHOTOGRAPHERS

Ralf Buscher
Dock 47, p066

Lukasz Chrobok
Sleeping Dogs, p026

**David Burghardt/
db-photo.de**
Moondoo, p035

Andrea Flak
20Up Skyline Bar, p041

Joachim Fliegner
Weserburg, pp102-103

Roland Halbe
Unilever HQ and Marco
Polo Tower, p067

Åke E:son Lindman
Müritzeum, p097

Peartree Digital
Monkey 47 gin, p073

Silke Schmidt
Tanzende Türme, p012
25hours HafenCity, p017
Henri Hotel, p018, p019
The George, p022

East, p023
Klippkroog, p025
Deichtorhallen, p027
Clouds, p031
Idol Bar, p033
Nil, p034
Henssler & Henssler,
pp036-037
Kaffee Elbgold, p040
Anna Sgroi, p042, p043
Die Bank, pp044-045
Cornelia Poletto, p047
Weltbühne, p050
Hoch3, p051
Bullerei, pp052-053
Johanna Brinckman, p055
Energiebunker, pp058-059
Floating Homes,
pp064-065
Spiegel HQ, p070
Elbphilharmonie, p071
Dorothea Schlueter, p077
Ply, pp078-079
The Box, p080, p081
Roomservice, p085
Lys Vintage, pp086-087
Aspria Spa, p089
Imtech Arena, pp090-091

Patrick Voigt
Dockland, pp010-011
Chilehaus, p013
Congress Center, p057

Elbberg Campus, p062
Köhlbrandbrücke, p063
Staatsoper, pp068-069

Markus Wendler
Hamburg city view,
inside front cover
Flakturm IV, pp014-015
Sandtorkai, pp028-029
Bistrot Vienna, p030
Tide, pp038-039
Café Paris, p046
A Mora, pp048-049
ADA 1, p060
Koppel 66, pp074-075
Anna Fuchs, pp082-083
D'Or, p084

HAMBURG
A COLOUR-CODED GUIDE TO THE HOT 'HOODS

EIMSBÜTTEL
A tree-lined residential district that is becoming increasingly hip as creatives take root

ST GEORG
This bohemian enclave has plenty of nightlife options and boating on the Aussenalster

MITTE WEST
Cultured central Hamburg is a mix of retail, cafés and the Planten un Blomen gardens

EPPENDORF/HARVESTEHUDE
The well-to-do haven of swanky villas is also a draw for its coterie of upmarket boutiques

HAFENCITY
Intensive docklands redevelopment and investment here is invigorating the entire city

SCHANZE
As entrepreneurs open stores and eateries, this alternative district is growing in stature

MITTE EAST
Swathes of clinker-brick office buildings characterise Hamburg's most historic hub

ALTONA/ST PAULI
From modern architecture to strip clubs to foodie delights, this is a multifaceted zone

For a full description of each neighbourhood, see the Introduction.
Featured venues are colour-coded, according to the district in which they are located.